ALLEN CARR

THE ILLUSTRATED EASY WAY FOR

WOMEN TO STOP SMOKING

I'M FREE!!

A LIBERATING GUIDE TO A SMOKE-FREE FUTURE

ARCTURUS

This book is dedicated to Afsoon

ARCTURUS

This edition published in 2013 by Arcturus Publishing Limited
26/27 Bickels Yard, 151–153 Bermondsey Street,
London SE1 3HA

ISBN: 978-1-78212-495-5
AD00035EN

Printed in the UK

CONTENTS

ABOUT EASYWAY

Allen Carr's hundred-cigarettes-a-day addiction was driving him to despair until, in 1983, after countless failed attempts to quit, he finally discovered what the world had been waiting for – the EASY WAY TO STOP SMOKING.

His network of clinics now spans the globe, operating in more than 150 cities in over 45 countries. Contact details for these clinics are given at the end of this book along with a discount voucher redeemable when booking a session at any UK/Worldwide Allen Carr's Easyway Clinic (you won't need it yourself – but you are welcome to pass it on to a friend who might appreciate it). The clinics offer a genuine money-back guarantee based on which the success rate is over 90 per cent.

Allen Carr's Easyway To Stop Smoking method is also available in regular book form, e-book format, CD audio book, digital audio book, webcast seminar, video on demand, iPhone + android apps, and DVD.

For details of these items, and other books which successfully apply Allen Carr's EASYWAY method to 'alcohol', 'weight control', 'fear of flying','worry', 'debt', and 'gambling' visit www.allencarr.com

BEFORE WE BEGIN...

If you've ever contemplated stopping smoking (and which smoker hasn't?) you will probably be under the illusion that it's DIFFICULT and that enormous WILLPOWER is required.

The name 'Easyway' should be a clue that this is not so.

This method enables you to 'GET IT' so that you can free yourself from the desire to smoke, quickly and easily.

RELAX!

READ ON and, by the end of this book, you'll

GET IT!

All you have to do is apply the following instructions...

INSTRUCTIONS

1. KEEP AN OPEN MIND

2. BE HAPPY ABOUT FREEING YOURSELF

3. DON'T JUMP THE GUN

4. WRITE A PERSONAL STATEMENT ABOUT YOUR GOAL AND KEEP IT VISIBLE

YOU'VE COME A LONG WAY, BABY!

**Oh dear, you *have* come a
long way, baby!**

Mind if I ask you something...?

...you consider yourself a LIBERATED woman, don't you?

You THINK for yourself…

…YOU decide where your own
life is heading…

...and you make your own
INDEPENDENT CHOICES?

Really? Good for you!

Then, wouldn't you say that, by definition,
being LIBERATED means you're FREE?

Then why do you NEED to SMOKE?

Oh, REALLY?

So does that mean that you can equally CHOOSE *not* to smoke?

THE ILLUSTRATED

OK then – CHOOSE to stop RIGHT NOW!

It's OK – you don't have to stop yet
(we'll get to that later)...

Remember – you can
keep smoking
until you
GET IT.

Don't worry – just keep
reading and you *will*
GET IT!

*ALL YOU HAVE TO DO
IS RELAX AND FOLLOW
THE
INSTRUCTIONS.*

Oh, so you don't like being CONTROLLED and MANIPULATED?

Do you *REALLY?*

If you had the CHOICE, you would choose to be a
NON-SMOKER – that's why you're reading this.
We all know that smoking's UNHEALTHY, FILTHY and
COSTS A FORTUNE. So why do you do it?

What do you actually find ENJOYABLE
about smoking?

But HOW does smoking actually HELP those things?

WELL, I'M NOT *EXACTLY* SURE *HOW* IT DOES THAT...

...ALL I KNOW IS THAT I FEEL *TENSE* WHEN I GO WITHOUT!

Can I ask you something else?

Are you GLAD that you smoke?

And if you had (or have) children, would you encourage
THEM to smoke?

And if you ENJOY smoking, why have
you picked up a book on QUITTING?

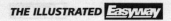

So obviously, there is a DILEMMA here: you want to SMOKE but you want to QUIT!

You're not alone in this.

In fact, every smoker goes through this same experience of being pulled in
TWO TOTALLY OPPOSITE DIRECTIONS...

TORN BETWEEN TWO LOVERS

You know you need to quit but you want to smoke.

It's like being torn between two LOVERS.

One is TEMPTING
but DANGEROUS...

...and the other is
a great guy but
not as
EXCITING.

Both keep whispering in your ear and each has
COMPELLING ARGUMENTS

You end up feeling CONFUSED and STUCK.
You know the GOOD GUY is best for you,
but you can't resist the BAD BOY.

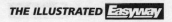

He makes such
TANTALIZING PROMISES,
you can't resist...

You KNOW these PROMISES are LIES!
After all, he's let you down time and time again.

Eventually, you're completely
FED UP with him...

...and you decide it's
time to LEAVE him, once
and for all!

But then all it takes
is ONE CALL...

...and you're right back
where you STARTED!

I CAN'T BELIEVE
I'VE GONE
BACK TO HIM!

You decide that you're just
too STUPID or WEAK
to get out of this...

Can you see the same pattern in your SMOKING?

In the same way that you feel dependent on the BAD BOY,
you believe that you simply can't live
without cigarettes.

Believe it or not, when it comes to stopping smoking, you don't need WILLPOWER.

Many people are under the same illusion (we'll reveal all shortly)…

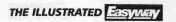

Just as WILLPOWER does not necessarily help you quit,
nor do INTELLIGENCE, COURAGE or STRENGTH
of CHARACTER necessarily
make any difference.

There are many AMAZING, SUCCESSFUL WOMEN who
have been addicted to SMOKING...

Bette Davis

Lucille Ball

Golda Meir

Virginia Woolf

But the question is, were they ADMIRED for their
ADDICTION, or their TALENTS and ACHIEVEMENTS?

LOOK— I KNOW IT'S *BAD* FOR ME! BUT WHY CAN'T I JUST *STOP?!*

The GOOD NEWS

is that you *CAN!*

But first you need to understand the nature of your ADDICTION to nicotine...

THE EVIL SPELL
OF ADDICTION

Oh, so you don't think you're an ADDICT?

Have you ever 'BORROWED' someone else's cigarettes?

Have you ever smoked BUTTS?

If your BRAND was out of stock, would you go WITHOUT?

Do you feel ASHAMED or EMBARRASSED about being a SMOKER?

Have you BROKEN PROMISES to yourself and others that you'll quit?

Have you LIED about the number of cigarettes you really smoke?

If you ran out, to
what LENGTHS
would you go
to get
CIGARETTES?

Have you ever done
something you're
not PROUD of
because of smoking?

Have you ever
MADE EXCUSES
for
HEALTH
PROBLEMS
caused by
SMOKING?

Do you try to
HIDE the fact that
you smoke?

So you LIE about it to yourself and others, COMPROMISE
yourself and go to extreme lengths to get your FIX.
Doesn't that sound like an ADDICT?

37

Smokers do not CHOOSE to smoke.

Once trapped, you have no CONTROL over your SMOKING.

Let's meet her.

Sophie must be EXHAUSTED. She has to exercise that CONTROL over and over and over again, every day of her life.

We all start off believing we have CONTROL
over our smoking.

The idea of it being a problem that will ruin our life doesn't
even occur to us. We're convinced that we'll be able to stop
when the time is right.

But when IS the right time?
When you can't BREATHE?
When you've RUINED your COMPLEXION?
When your HEART fails?
When you get CANCER?

Somehow, that 'SOMEDAY'
never quite arrives, does it?

Sophie's need to exercise CONTROL requires WILLPOWER, which is constantly tested…

…and this creates TENSION.

Using WILLPOWER creates MENTAL CONFLICT which increases the craving for whatever you feel you are being DEPRIVED of.

You may hold out for a while, but you still feel as though you are MISSING something.

The more you try to RESIST the TEMPTATION, the more OBSESSED you become by the CRAVING.

The very thing that you want to be rid of is the thing that is UPPERMOST in your mind.

In the end, WILLPOWER keeps you HOOKED
on cigarettes because
all your FOCUS is on what you feel you are MISSING.

This is also why SUBSTITUTES
DO NOT WORK – particularly
those containing NICOTINE.

They just swap one form
of the drug for another,
therefore prolonging
the addiction.

Feeling constantly DEPRIVED does NOT make a HAPPY
NON-SMOKER, which is what you want to be!

Now, let's take a good look at how addiction works.

Becoming addicted to cigarettes is like
falling for a sinister form of SEDUCTION.

To demonstrate this, let's go back to our BAD BOY example.

Here you are, living your life quite happily
without attachment. You are independent, free and in
control of your own destiny...

...then one fateful day, you meet this DANGEROUS, but ATTRACTIVE type.

At first, you're not all that INTERESTED. You're CURIOUS but not really TEMPTED.

After all, this guy has TROUBLE written all over him!

And you know you're way too SENSIBLE to fall for such a type.

However, there is something
strangely COMPELLING
about him...

...that eventually
becomes
IRRESISTIBLE.

Once you've fallen
for him, you can't
bear being APART...

...that is, until one day
you come to the
SHOCKING
REALIZATION...

...that this relationship is actually doing you great HARM.

The rose-tinted glasses come off. You begin to HATE everything about him...

...and decide that you want OUT.

But strangely, you can't quite let him go. He has you under his SPELL...

...so you IGNORE the PROBLEMS...

...and try to block the DANGERS from your mind.

Not only this
but you find that
all exits are now
BARRED…

It's no use. You no longer have a CHOICE.
You've become a SLAVE to his demands.

You're STUCK in this love-hate relationship…

…TILL **DEATH** DO YOU PART!

NO!

As if this wasn't BAD enough,
this union has produced
some very unpleasant
offspring…

THE
TERRIBLE
TWINS

THE BIRTH OF TWIN MONSTERS

This sinister pair run riot through your life from the moment you start your relationship with CIGARETTES.

Once you are hooked, they ensure that you remain hooked, because their very survival depends on this.

They are UGLY, DEVIOUS, CUNNING AND CONTROLLING.

They are

THE
SMOKING
MONSTERS!

TWIN NUMBER ONE
is in charge of

BRAINWASHING.

He is the BIG monster.

He is the voice in your head that convinces you
that you NEED to smoke and that you cannot COPE
without cigarettes.

TWIN NUMBER TWO
is responsible for the feelings of

NICOTINE WITHDRAWAL.

He is the LITTLE monster.

He creates those EMPTY, INSECURE
feelings that trigger your desire for your next fix and
ensure that you keep TOPPING UP the supply of nicotine
in your system.

The SMOKING MONSTERS
have complete
CONTROL over you…

The BRAINWASHER
NAGS at you
incessantly…

…and the
CRAVER
keeps you
constantly
on EDGE.

Their demands are never-ending...

...and even while you continue to smoke, they are
NEVER, EVER satisfied!

You end up thinking that cigarettes
must have some special hold over you.

Why else would you keep SMOKING?

This LOVE-HATE relationship is tearing you apart.
You wish you were FREE of them, and yet you THINK
you NEED them!

This is the most SINISTER part of
the TRAP.

You have fallen
for the TRICKERY...

...you are HYPNOTIZED by an ILLUSION
that makes you THINK...

...that you can't GET BY WITHOUT THEM!

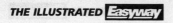

So, how do you explode a MYTH?

You expose the TRICKERY behind it.

THE ONLY DIFFERENCE BETWEEN A SMOKER AND A NON-SMOKER IS...

THE NON-SMOKER HAS NO *DESIRE*
TO SMOKE!

Well, here's an interesting fact – *you are ALREADY*
a non-smoker UNLESS you LIGHT ANOTHER ONE!

What if you no longer had any DESIRE to smoke?

It's only the BRAINWASHING MONSTER convincing you that you need to smoke…

Once the BRAINWASHING MONSTER is defeated, the PHYSICAL CRAVINGS are MINOR!

After all, there is no PHYSICAL PAIN!

It's time to TAKE HIM ON!

GETTING
THE KIDS
TO LEAVE
HOME

TWIN NUMBER ONE is the main one running the show. In fact, once we effectively deal with him, the other guy is reduced to a mere squeak.

This twin, the BRAINWASHER, has you totally convinced that smoking is actually HELPFUL to you in some way and that you will be DEPRIVED of a PLEASURE if you stop smoking.

Let's start by taking a good, hard look at:

THE PLEASURES OF SMOKING

Gee, isn't smoking FUN?

Don't you get a real KICK out of...

...the COUGH...

...the DISDAIN...

...the SMELL...

...the WRINKLES...

...the HEALTH
SCARES...

KATHUMP! KATHUMP!

...the COST...

...the PALE COMPLEXION...

...and, of course, the ENDLESS GUILT?

Every day, you are
confronted by the REALITY
that smoking is
RUNNING and RUINING
your ENTIRE LIFE.

BUT I KNOW
ALL THIS!

THEN WHY
DOESN'T THIS
MAKE ME
STOP?!

Because you are STILL
under the ILLUSION
that there is something
to MISS about smoking
and that you won't be able
to COPE without it.

You have been CONNED into thinking that SMOKING
provides you with some sort of
PLEASURE or CRUTCH.

69

Let's take a look at the times when smoking seems to provide genuine RELIEF:

THE 'FAVOURITE' CIGARETTES

1. THE FIRST ONE OF THE DAY

2. AFTER EXERCISE

3. DURING BREAKS

4. AFTER MEALS

5. WITH A DRINK

What is actually happening here is that usually there has been a LONG GAP since your last NICOTINE FIX, and so the relief seems even more precious.

In these cases, you have made a mental ASSOCIATION between smoking and satisfying your HUNGER or THIRST.

In the end, it SEEMS that you can't enjoy these things without smoking.

BUT what is really happening is that you feel 'better' only because you are

FEEDING YOUR NEED FOR A FIX!

THE ONE AND ONLY 'PLEASURE' TO BE DERIVED FROM SMOKING IS THE RELIEF OF TOPPING UP YOUR DROPPING NICOTINE SUPPLY.

In fact, you actually feel WORSE!

It may *seem* that way – as part of the illusion – but each time you 'top up' you *actually* keep yourself on a constant downward spiral.

Let's look at how this works.

Say this is you at your best
BEFORE you ever started
SMOKING...

...then, that
FATEFUL DAY –
the arrival of the
TERRIBLE TWINS!

73

The LITTLE MONSTER soon develops an ENORMOUS APPETITE...

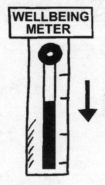

...and when he's HUNGRY, you immediately feel STRESSED.

His highly protective brother convinces you that ALL WILL BE WELL if you just keep FEEDING that hunger...

...and, indeed, this seems to be true, because the LITTLE MONSTER immediately settles down when you have a cigarette.

But it's not long before he's HUNGRY again and, once more, you experience that INSECURE, HOLLOW feeling...

75

...and with that, your
WELLBEING takes
another NOSEDIVE.

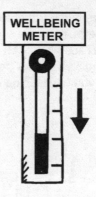

Yet again, you
FEED him,
just to get
some peace...

...but it's SHORT-LIVED...

...and you can hardly believe it when
he's DEMANDING
to be FED again!

THERE IS *NO END* TO THIS HUNGER
YOU CAN *NEVER, EVER* FEED IT ENOUGH
TO STOP THE CRAVING.

You could smoke a MILLION, TRILLION CIGARETTES
and still crave 'JUST ONE MORE'!

And, while you continue to smoke, you will NEVER,
EVER reach the level of WELLBEING you experienced
before you smoked.

Having to CONSTANTLY
FEED THE CRAVING means
that you feel:

MORE STRESSED, MORE OFTEN...

...and your WELLBEING eventually
PLUMMETS

LOWER and LOWER.

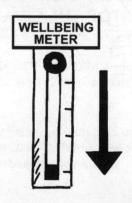

WHAT DOES SMOKING DO FOR YOU?

NOTHING

OK, clearly we need to EXPLODE some more MYTHS.

EXCUSE ME, MYTH!

THE ILLUSTRATED **Easyway**

We understand. The TWINS don't give up easily without a fight.

After all, they've been running the show for a long time now.

So, let's address those lingering ILLUSIONS...

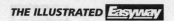

What are your lingering CONCERNS about quitting?

WELL, YOU PUT ON *WEIGHT*, DON'T YOU? I'D HATE TO GET *FAT*!

You'll only GAIN WEIGHT if you EAT MORE and you'll only eat more if you use food as a SUBSTITUTE for smoking.

You'll only need a SUBSTITUTE if you are still holding on to the idea that you're MISSING SOMETHING!

Once your body has managed to clear out all that GUNGE, you'll find ENERGY in abundance and you're more likely to be ACTIVE!

LOOK, OUT! COMING THROUGH!

You'll probably end up FITTER than you've been for ages!

Why would *ONE PARTICULAR CIGARETTE* taste better than the others?

WHAT ABOUT THE ONE AFTER A MEAL? I'LL MISS THAT!

YUMMY ONE!

BUT I REALLY DO *ENJOY* THE *TASTE!*

It's the ASSOCIATIONS you make between the pleasure of eating and the cigarette afterwards, that cons you into thinking that it tastes better.

In fact, you make these same ASSOCIATIONS
with other pleasures, such as:

a cup of COFFEE or TEA...

... alcohol...

...socializing...

...and, well,
YOU-KNOW-WHAT!

Remember that it's the ASSOCIATION you make between
TOPPING UP YOUR FIX, at the same time as you are
SATISFYING other needs, that
confuses you into thinking that the cigarette is a PLEASURE.

All you need do is
remember just how BAD
cigarettes tasted when
you started smoking, to
realize that this
'pleasure' is an
ILLUSION!

The only thing that makes
a cigarette taste 'GOOD'
is that, without it,
you experience the
discomfort of the
CRAVING for your FIX.

= GROWL! =

Maybe, but neither involves any PHYSICAL PAIN, and
HUNGER is a NATURAL signal
to alert you to take in SUSTENANCE.

It protects your SURVIVAL.

NICOTINE CRAVINGS are ARTIFICIAL ALARMS created only
because you are dependent on a DRUG.

These ensure your DESTRUCTION.

86

EATING IS A *NATURAL* ACT
DESIGNED TO KEEP YOU
ALIVE AND WELL.

SMOKING IS AN UNNATURAL
ACT DESIGNED ONLY TO
FEED AN ADDICTION.

EATING <u>SATISFIES</u> HUNGER.

SMOKING <u>CREATES</u> *MORE* HUNGER.

Remember:
this HUNGER
has
NO END!

If that's really true, your life should be TOTAL BLISS!

REALLY? Then you should be
TOTALLY STRESS-FREE, COMPLETELY RELAXED,
NEVER BORED and ABLE TO CONCENTRATE FULLY
all of the time!

NON-SMOKERS experience the same STRESSES and life CHALLENGES as SMOKERS, but smoking ADDS an EXTRA STRESS that is totally UNNECESSARY!

Let's look at this a little more closely by examining a stressful situation:

A JOB INTERVIEW

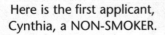

Here is the first applicant, Cynthia, a NON-SMOKER.

And here is Jayne, who SMOKES.

On the morning of the interview, Cynthia only has to deal with her pre-interview NERVES...

...while Jayne has already had to deal with an extra STRESS...

Her LITTLE MONSTER needs a FIX...
...and she's
OUT OF CIGARETTES!

Later, Cynthia has only to sit out the STRESS of waiting to be called in for the interview...

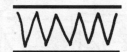

STRESS OF INTERVIEW

...while poor Jayne has to deal with this as well as the STRESS of not being able to SMOKE!

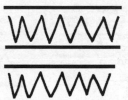

STRESS OF WANTING CIGARETTE

STRESS OF INTERVIEW

Finally, the interview is over and this brings RELIEF...

...well, at least it does
for Cynthia...

STRESS OF INTERVIEW

...Jayne still has to FEED
HER MONSTER!

STRESS OF WANTING CIGARETTE

STRESS OF INTERVIEW

The STRESS on the smoker involves
CONSTANTLY meeting the
ENDLESS DEMANDS of trying
to keep the CRAVINGS at bay.

SMOKING DOES NOT *RELIEVE* STRESS-IT *CREATES* EXTRA STRESS!

Not only is this
STRESSFUL, but it is hard
to CONCENTRATE
when there is the
constant
DISTRACTION
of the cravings.

I CAN'T THINK STRAIGHT! I NEED A SMOKE!

This leads to another
ILLUSION –
that smoking
ASSISTS
CONCENTRATION.

BUT I FIND I CAN CONCENTRATE BETTER WHEN I SMOKE!

SMOKING only SEEMS to
help because without
cigarettes, your mind is DISTRACTED by the craving and it
only SEEMS to relieve boredom because, when you're bored,
you become aware of the
itch and want to scratch it
by lighting up.

LOOK, I ACTUALLY ENJOY SMOKING! DON'T I DESERVE A TREAT NOW AND THEN?

You had to really
WORK at
being addicted
to cigarettes.

93

It wasn't PLEASURABLE at the start, was it?

Light one now, and take six deep puffs and then analyze what you are actually 'ENJOYING' about it.

HMMM... I FEEL A BIT SICK!

OH, I WEAR *TIGHT SHOES* BECAUSE IT'S SUCH A *HUGE RELIEF* TO TAKE THEM *OFF!*

The only 'pleasure' in smoking is trying to relieve the empty, insecure feeling of nicotine withdrawal which is caused by the nicotine itself.

This is a common illusion. It's not a matter of keeping your hands busy – again it's the need to feed the LITTLE MONSTER!

THINK ABOUT IT. If it really was just about giving you something to do, you could simply fiddle with the cigarette.

Instead, you PUT IT IN YOUR MOUTH, LIGHT IT and INHALE. What has keeping your hands busy got to do with it?

The same goes for the sense of ORAL GRATIFICATION. You might satisfy that by putting the cigarette in your mouth, but why LIGHT it?

Why INHALE?

Would you PANIC if you ran out of CHEESE?
You might miss it, but doing without for a while wouldn't
fill you with ANXIETY.

Even if you ADORE cheese
(or any other food),
do you need to carry
a supply with you
everywhere to avoid
PANICKING?

Get it CLEAR in your mind: the cigarette
CAUSES the feeling of panic! Stop smoking and you'll
get rid of it PERMANENTLY!

Cigarettes are the WORST ENEMY you'll ever have!
Would you willingly stay home with someone who makes
you a slave, takes your money and kills you?

What is the RITUAL for?
It's just what you need to
do to get the drug into
your system.

Think about it.
Would you still
perform the same actions if you
didn't need the NICOTINE?
You'd find it plain STUPID!

What would happen if you took that phone call WITHOUT smoking? Is the phone DANGEROUS?
Will you not be able to SPEAK or HEAR?

It's like Pavlov's dog, which was trained to associate hunger with the ring of a bell – when a phone rings, it's a TRIGGER for you to smoke.

It's the BRAINWASHING, not the PHONE CALL.

So, you've decided to SPEED UP the process? Smoking is SUICIDE. How do you want YOUR future to be?

Dying prematurely from smoking is bad enough, but even worse are the DISTRESS, PAIN and TORTURE of smoking-related illnesses and the YEARS of suffering these cause.

Are you starting to see how DELUDED you have been by the
BRAINWASHING?

Your thinking has been totally
MANIPULATED by your
ADDICTION to NICOTINE.

The BRAINWASHER has
made you abandon your
REASON, and lose your
INDEPENDENCE and
FREEDOM.

So who's REALLY
in charge of your life...?

YOU or these TERRIBLE MONSTERS?

SECRET WOMEN'S BUSINESS

STILL not convinced?

There are some remaining issues that are of particular
concern to women, which need to be
explored further. Let's address these now.

Despite all the changes in modern times, it's not easy being
a woman. We've had to fight for our rights and we have to
fight to keep them.

Actually, there's even more pressure now that so many
women are balancing careers, motherhood, relationships,
health and lifestyle.

In many ways
we have to be
SUPERWOMEN...

I FEEL SO *STRESSED* ALL THE TIME!

Feeling STRESSED is one of the most common EXCUSES for not stopping smoking.

You may make a solemn oath that you will stop...

THAT'S IT!!

I'M DOING OK...

...you may do fine for a while...

...then SOMETHING HAPPENS and you reach for your old 'FRIEND'.

IT'S OVER!

But surely you can see that this is no 'FRIEND'!

Let's leave out a letter and you have the REAL picture!

FIEND

This 'FRIEND' doesn't give a DAMN about you.
This 'FRIEND' is COSTING you a FORTUNE. This 'FRIEND' is
CONTROLLING you like a SLAVE. This 'FRIEND' is KILLING YOU.

And what is this 'FRIEND' doing for you?
NOTHING!

Life, for EVERYONE, involves UPS and DOWNS, GAINS and LOSSES.

Why complicate it further with the EXTRA burden of FEEDING the FIEND?

By the way – what made you START smoking?

and NOW...?

 and NOW...?

and NOW...?

How VALID are these reasons now?

Look, we've all made some DUMB decisions –
that's part of life – but whatever made you start smoking
is IRRELEVANT NOW.

WHAT MATTERS is
WHAT COMES
NEXT.

You are doing your best in the
HARDEST JOB IN THE WORLD.

The trouble is, SMOKING is ADDING to your STRESS.
And, let's be honest, smoking can only ever UNDERMINE
all of your attempts to be a good parent.

There's the SHAME...

...the
GUILT...

...the COST...

...the LACK OF ENERGY...

...and the DANGERS.

These are extra, terrible, UNNECESSARY
BURDENS that make your job HARDER.

Wouldn't you find motherhood more enjoyable
if you had more ENERGY and the
PEACE of MIND of being FREE of SMOKING?

One of the things that is of concern to most women (rightly or wrongly) is APPEARANCE.

We are bombarded with messages about beauty at every turn.

Just for a moment, see yourself as a non-smoker sees you.

Not too PRETTY, is it?

While you're at it, take a look at other SMOKERS. Do they look HAPPY to be smoking?

Research has shown that smokers are more irritable, anxious and depressed than non-smokers.

Is a smoker PROUD about reeking of cigarette smoke or the way smoking makes her feel?

IT'S CALLED EAU DU CIG!

As we all know, beauty is only SKIN DEEP and smoking can wreck your looks faster than anything.

ON THE OUTSIDE

The lack of oxygen and the clogging of blood vessels ages you well before your time:

GREY COMPLEXION

DRY SKIN

LINES AND WRINKLES

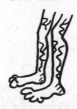

VARICOSE VEINS

DULL EYES

YELLOW TEETH

ON THE INSIDE

LUNG DAMAGE

LIVER DAMAGE

THE RISK OF
GANGRENE

HEART PROBLEMS

POSSIBLE
STROKE

CLOGGING UP
OF VEINS AND
ARTERIES

...that's just FOR STARTERS.

But you KNOW all this, too, don't you?

OF COURSE I DO! THE WARNINGS ARE EVERYWHERE!

So if you know the DANGERS,
WHY have you continued to smoke?

If you look back at the reasons why you started smoking, you will see that, at the heart of needing to FIT IN, BE ACKNOWLEDGED, BE REBELLIOUS, BE INDEPENDENT, there is A FEELING that you, as you are,

ARE NOT ENOUGH.

We are constantly
BRAINWASHED
into thinking
that we need some
miraculous device,
gadget, remedy or drug
to be complete.

Think about the times you are most prone to light up.
These are usually the times when you feel INSECURE,
INADEQUATE or OVERWHELMED.

You have been FOOLED into thinking that the cigarette provides relief, but it's an ILLUSION. All you're trying to do is get rid of the craving for nicotine.

What you are REALLY aiming for is to GET BACK to feeling like a NON-SMOKER, who NEVER suffers from nicotine withdrawal in the first place.

It's time to LOVE YOURSELF, VALUE YOURSELF and HEAL YOURSELF.

You have put others' needs first all your life.

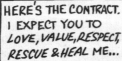

You have DOUBTED yourself, NEGLECTED yourself and, worst of all, HOPED that someone or something else would FIX you.

But you will only be VALUED if you VALUE YOURSELF.

NO-ONE
and
NO THING
FORCES
you to smoke.

Now you KNOW the TRUTH about the TRAP
of ADDICTION, it's YOUR CHOICE.

WHAT'S IT TO BE?

GEE, TOUGH CHOICE!

A LIFETIME OF COST, SLAVERY AND ILL HEALTH WITH NO BENEFITS WHATSOEVER

FREEDOM, PEACE, MONEY, WELLBEING AND HEALTH

What would be the LOVING thing to do for yourself?

YOU *ARE WORTHY* OF BEING
HEALTHY, HAPPY and FREE!

Now for the
GOOD NEWS.

Once you stop smoking, it is only a matter of HOURS before
nicotine leaves your system.

Your body is a
MAGNIFICENT,
SELF-CORRECTING
mechanism
which IMMEDIATELY
sets about
REPAIRING the
damage.

In fact, it's a wonder that your body copes with
smoking at all!

If you injected the
nicotine from
JUST ONE CIGARETTE
directly into your vein,
it would KILL YOU.

That's not to mention the thousands of toxins and chemicals
(including rat poison!) in each cigarette.

IT'S TIME TO

GET REAL!

SMOKING WILL NEVER, EVER
MAKE YOU FEEL WHOLE

SMOKING IS *MISERY*

THERE IS *NOTHING* TO MISS!

THERE IS *EVERYTHING* TO GAIN!

NOW YOU KNOW THE TRUTH
WHY **ON EARTH** WOULD YOU KEEP SMOKING?!

HERE'S SOME MORE OF WHAT YOU CAN LOOK FORWARD
TO WHEN YOU'RE A NON-SMOKER:

You'll gain
new self-respect

You'll feel more
confident

You'll no longer
be a slave

That black shadow
of fear will be gone

And LIFE WILL BE INFINITELY BETTER ALL ROUND!

KICKING OUT
JUNIOR

OK, now we've dealt with the BIG MONSTER,
THE BRAINWASHER,
handling the LITTLE MONSTER –
THE PHYSICAL WITHDRAWALS –
will be a cinch.

Of COURSE
he's going to COMPLAIN for a
few days when you cut
off his SUPPLY!

He's being
DEPRIVED and he
HATES that!

He's used to having
his way. He's not
used to you saying NO.

He may even
throw a
TANTRUM
or TWO!

122

He'll TRY *ANYTHING* to get a FIX!

He'll FLIRT...

...he'll MOAN...

...he'll PRETEND
to CARE about you...

...he'll even BEG.

So, WHAT TO DO?

Well, instead of thinking of this as...

...see this as a POSITIVE SIGN that the NIGHTMARE is finally ending.

The monster is making a fuss because he is DYING! (Don't worry: withdrawal symptoms are noticeable for less than a week.)

You are going to STARVE HIM TO DEATH.

124

What should you do?

REJOICE!

IT'S **OVER!**

YOU WILL NEVER, EVER HAVE TO GO
THROUGH THE OLD FEAR, DOUBT
AND STRUGGLE AGAIN.

YOU'VE WON!!!

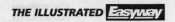
PREPARING
TO LAUNCH

CONGRATULATIONS!

You are about to RECLAIM YOUR LIFE.

10... You are about to LAUNCH YOURSELF into CLEAN, FRESH AIR.

9... You are about to make the BEST DECISION of your life.

8... You are about to liberate yourself FOREVER from the PRISON of smoking.

You are about to be...

FREE!!

Of course, it's NATURAL to feel a bit APPREHENSIVE at this point. You're embarking on a whole new way of being. But NEVER, EVER doubt that this is the BEST DECISION you will have ever made.

All you need is to JUST DO IT.
That will be all the proof you need.

HOWEVER, IF YOU STILL BELIEVE:

That you're making some sort of 'sacrifice'

That you'll keep a small supply around 'just in case'

That 'just one' won't hurt

That smoking serves you in any way

That you can 'control' your smoking

That you'd be better off smoking than quitting...

– THEN YOU'RE NOT READY.
YOU HAVEN'T 'GOT IT'.

GO BACK AND READ THE BOOK AGAIN.
THINK ABOUT IT. MAKE NOTES.

DO NOT MISS THIS CHANCE TO BE FREE!

READY?

YOU BET!

GREAT!

Here are your final instructions before TAKE OFF:

<u>BE ALERT TO THE LITTLE MONSTER'S TRICKS</u>

DO NOT UNDERESTIMATE
THIS GUY!
He's no FRIEND
of yours! He's robbed
you of years of peace,
vitality and wellbeing
and he'll never stop until
he KILLS you or you KILL him.

YOU MUST NEVER, EVER OPEN THE DOOR TO HIM AGAIN!

<u>APPROACH QUITTING
WITH ELATION</u>

Check your attitude.
This is a GOOD thing!
Why would you RESENT it?
NOTHING *BAD*
IS HAPPENING!
Be HAPPY about it!

DON'T AVOID SMOKERS OR SMOKING SITUATIONS.

Go out and enjoy social occasions as usual, even if you're surrounded by smokers. Realize they are the ones being DEPRIVED – not you!

DON'T ENVY SMOKERS

Why would you envy someone who is still imprisoned? You know what? They envy YOU!

<u>REMEMBER, THERE IS
NO SUCH THING AS
'JUST ONE' CIGARETTE</u>

If you light up 'just one',
you create a craving for
another and another and
another...

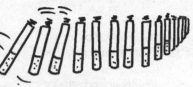

FEED IT ONCE AND THAT CRAVING WILL <u>NEVER</u> END!

<u>**DON'T PUT OFF
BECOMING A
NON-SMOKER**</u>

You are a non-smoker the
MINUTE you stop
feeding the monster.

TO BECOME A NON-SMOKER JUST DON'T *EVER* LIGHT ANOTHER CIGARETTE!

DON'T WORRY IF YOU STILL THINK ABOUT SMOKING FOR A WHILE

As a NON-SMOKER, you'll still THINK about smoking

–

after all, it's been a major part of your life till now.

But you will need to think DIFFERENTLY about it.

THIS IS THE WAY TO THINK ABOUT IT:

THANK GOODNESS THAT'S OVER!!

Right – ready to go?

LET'S DO IT!

BLAST OFF!

THE RITUAL

At last, it's time!

You are about to smoke
YOUR LAST CIGARETTE!

We'll do this with a little RITUAL...

WHY DO I HAVE
TO DO A *RITUAL*?
I DON'T *WANT*
TO SMOKE
ANYMORE!

The ritual cements
your conviction that:

I WILL *NEVER*,
EVER SMOKE
AGAIN!!

If you've been smoking till now but have lost the desire to
smoke, here is your opportunity to prove it to yourself. If
you'd already stopped smoking for a few days, just take this
moment to confirm your decision NEVER to smoke again.

Now, LIGHT the last cigarette.

Really notice just how BAD it feels, how DISGUSTING it smells and think how it HURTS your precious body in so many, many ways.

Now, STUB OUT the cigarette
with a
FEELING OF PURE JOY!

Gather up EVERY SINGLE THING
to do with SMOKING and throw it
all away!

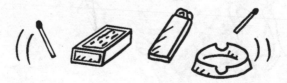

You might actually feel like dancing!

Go ahead!!!

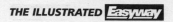
Now STRIP OFF those STINKING CLOTHES

Take a LONG,
LUXURIOUS BATH

WASH YOUR HAIR   CLEAN YOUR TEETH

SAVOUR how CLEAN and FRESH and FREE you feel!

NOW BLAST OFF
INTO LIFE...

...WONDER WOMAN!

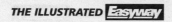

TELL ALLEN CARR'S EASYWAY ORGANISATION THAT YOU'VE ESCAPED

Leave a comment on *www.allencarr.com*, email
yippee@allencarr.com, like our Facebook page
www.facebook.com/AllenCarr
or write to the Worldwide Head Office address shown below.

ALLEN CARR'S EASYWAY CLINICS

The following list indicates the countries where Allen Carr's
Easyway To Stop Smoking Clinics are currently operational.
Check *www.allencarr.com* for latest additions to this list.
The success rate at the clinics, based on the three month
money-back guarantee, is over 90 per cent.

Selected clinics also offer sessions that deal with alcohol,
other drugs, and weight issues. Please check with your
nearest clinic, listed below, for details.

Allen Carr's Easyway guarantees that you will find it easy to
stop at the clinics or your money back.

ALLEN CARR'S EASYWAY
Worldwide Head Office
Park House, 14 Pepys Road, Raynes Park,
London SW20 8NH ENGLAND
Tel: +44 (0)208 9447761
Email: mail@allencarr.com
Website: www.allencarr.com

Worldwide Press Office
TEL: +44 (0)7970 88 44 52
Email: jd@allencarr.com

UK Clinic Information and Central Booking Line
0800 389 2115 (Freephone)

UNITED KINGDOM	GERMANY	NORWAY
REPUBLIC OF	GREECE	PERU
IRELAND	GUATEMALA	POLAND
AUSTRALIA	HONG KONG	PORTUGAL
AUSTRIA	HUNGARY	ROMANIA
BELGIUM	ICELAND	RUSSIA
BRAZIL	INDIA	SERBIA
BULGARIA	ISRAEL	SINGAPORE
CANADA	ITALY	SLOVENIA
CHILE	JAPAN	SOUTH AFRICA
COLOMBIA	LATVIA	SOUTH KOREA
CYPRUS	LEBANON	SPAIN
DENMARK	LITHUANIA	SWEDEN
ECUADOR	MAURITIUS	SWITZERLAND
ESTONIA	MEXICO	TURKEY
FINLAND	NETHERLANDS	UKRAINE
FRANCE	NEW ZEALAND	USA

Visit *www.allencarr.com* to access your nearest
clinic's contact details.

OTHER ALLEN CARR PUBLICATIONS

Allen Carr's revolutionary Easyway method is available in a
wide variety of formats, including digitally as audiobooks and
ebooks, and has been successfully applied to a broad range
of subjects.

For more information about Easyway publications, please visit
www.easywaypublishing.com

Allen Carr's Stop Smoking Now (with hypnotherapy CD)
ISBN: 978-1-84837-373-0

Stop Smoking with Allen Carr (with 70-minute audio CD)
ISBN: 978-1-84858-997-1

Allen Carr's Illustrated Easy Way to Stop Smoking
ISBN: 978-1-84837-930-5

Finally Free!
ISBN: 978-1-84858-979-7

Allen Carr's Easy Way for Women to Stop Smoking
ISBN: 978-1-84837-464-5

Allen Carr's How to Be a Happy Non-Smoker
ISBN: 978-0-572-03163-3

Allen Carr's Smoking Sucks (Parent Guide with 16 page pull-out comic)
ISBN: 978-0-572-03320-0

Allen Carr's No More Ashtrays
ISBN: 978-1-84858-083-1

Allen Carr's Little Book of Quitting
ISBN: 978-1-45490-242-3

Allen Carr's Only Way to Stop Smoking Permanently
ISBN: 978-0-14-024475-1

Allen Carr's Easy Way to Stop Smoking
ISBN: 978-0-71819-455-0

Allen Carr's How to Stop Your Child Smoking
ISBN: 978-0-14027-836-1

Allen Carr's Easy Way to Control Alcohol
ISBN: 978-1-84837-465-2

Allen Carr's No More Hangovers
ISBN: 978-1-84837-555-0

Allen Carr's Lose Weight Now (with hypnotherapy CD)
ISBN: 978-1-84837-720-2

Allen Carr's No More Diets
ISBN: 978-1-84837-554-3

Allen Carr's Easy Weigh to Lose Weight
ISBN: 978-0-14026-358-9

Allen Carr's Easy Way to Stop Gambling
ISBN: 978-1-78212-448-1

Allen Carr's No More Worrying
ISBN: 978-1-84837-826-1

Allen Carr's Get Out of Debt Now
ISBN: 978-1-84837-98-7

Allen Carr's Easy Way to Enjoy Flying
ISBN: 978-0-71819-458-3

Allen Carr's Burning Ambition
ISBN: 978-0-14103-030-2

Allen Carr's Packing It In The Easy Way (the autobiography)
ISBN: 978-0-14101-517-0

DISCOUNT VOUCHER
FOR
ALLEN CARR'S EASYWAY CLINICS

Recover the price of this book
when you attend an
Allen Carr's Easyway Clinic
anywhere in the world.

Allen Carr has a global network
of clinics where he guarantees
you will find it easy to stop
smoking or your money back.

The success rate based on this
money-back guarantee is over 90 per cent.

When you book your appointment
mention this voucher and you will
receive a discount on the value
of this book. Contact your
nearest clinic for more information
on how the sessions work and
to book your appointment.

Not valid in conjunction with any other offer.